# STAR Finder

## Anita Gibson

*Dear Petra,*
*You are a blessing*
*I love how you*
*love others!*
*Love ya*
*Anita*

**KP**

**KILGORE PUBLISHING**
**Flint Michigan**
**Since 2015**

**ISBN 978-0-9961347-8-1**
For Worldwide Distribution
Printed in the U.S.A.

# Prepare to

# Change Your

# Child's Life!

# Table Contents

*Dedication*
*Foreward by Mrs. Cymona Bolden*

The Problem ................................................... 1

Parents Are More Powerful Than They Think ........ 11

Schooling Should Not Be a Negative Experience .... 32

You Can't Pour from an Empty Cup ................... 39

How to Begin to Win ..................................... 51

What is STAR Finder? ................................... 61

Is Homeschool a Possibility for Your Child? .......... 75

How Can Your Organization Create Programs to Help

Students Succeed? ....................................... 88

*STAR Finder Strategies* ...................................92

*About the Author* ....................................... 95

# Dedication

This book is dedicated to all parents who know their child is struggling academically and are frustrated, trying to figure out what to do. I can empathize with your pain and understand how helpless, powerless and anxious you may feel at times. Your answers are in this book.

Glen, my dear husband you are my fortress. You have created a safe place for me to live, learn and love, and I will be forever grateful. Thank you to our precious children: Lauren, our valiant one; Dannielle, our precious nurturer; and Ricky, our sunshine. You gave your dad and me the privilege of learning how to help you grow and reach your full potential.

Rhonda Knight Boyle, my strengths coach, you were the one who ignited the strengths fire in me. You helped me to articulate what was always in my heart and encouraged me to keep gaining knowledge so I could help others. I cannot thank you enough.

Precious Brown, I thank you for all your publishing assistance. You kept me on task and encouraged me on days when I wasn't sure if I could get it done.

Aprille Hunt, you helped me to find my voice and my audience. Thank you for your kind and consistent support.

What an amazing business coach you are. You are the one that inspired me to believe that I could!

I am so thankful to God for ordering my steps because this journey is one that He has ordained and to which He has called me. I appreciate that God trusted me to assist parents in enabling their children to win academically. I pray that thousands of children's lives are forever changed.

Let the S.T.A.R. Finder Revolution BEGIN!

# Foreward

As a tutor and teacher at Shabach Christian Academy Homeschool and PXL Academy, I am honored to share that for the past ten years, Anita Gibson has been my friend, my employer and my family's educational coach. Anita is a true and faithful believer and instructor of the educational principles and information laid out in this book. I have personally witnessed with my two sons and numerous other family's children, the "fruit" of following her educational coaching strategies and techniques.

I can further testify that my son has significantly benefitted from the coaching we received from Anita, who helped me to become more aware of the need to develop an individualized program for each of my children. Understanding that my son is extremely artistic, she shared interactive and hands-on techniques to help him grasp the lessons. Under her guidance, I tailored his educational journey to his unique way of learning which resulted in improved academics and increased engagement with and interest in his education.

But my son is not the only one who needs these strategies. There are many students in our country who need diversified academic solutions to enable them to succeed. Anita's focus on observing each child's strengths and weaknesses and developing a tailor-made learning pathway is essential to the success of our students, our communities and our society.

I believe that if you read this book and utilize the strategies and principles in it, you will be encouraged, enlightened, and equipped to assist both your children and others in achieving their academic potential.

*Mrs. Cymona Bolden*

"Every child is a STAR! Each of them have been gifted by God to be great at something. Sometimes you can see what it is right away, sometimes you must dig a little." ~ *Mrs. Anita Gibson*

## *Chapter 1*

Our country understands that students learn in many ways. Our government has put initiatives in place to respond to the concerns we have about children being "left behind" academically. But despite its good intentions, we find ourselves still trying to find effective solutions for many students whose needs are not being met in public, charter and/or private educational environments.

The students know something is different about them, they know they learn differently. But they think the problem is with them; which has a negative impact on their self-esteem and confidence levels. They are told that they can do well in school; that they just need to be more focused. If they just study harder and longer, they will be fine. Well, they <u>have</u> tried, and it's still not working.

Unfortunately, our children are made to feel that the only reason that success is not attainable is their fault. No one wants to acknowledge to these children that the academic environment is the primary cause of the problem. The teachers must focus on teaching to the test, classroom sizes are increasing and students are taught in ways that don't engage them, etc. This causes student's perspective about academics to become decidedly negative, which

1

causes them to shut down, not engage in various academic subjects, become disruptive, bored, unfocused and sometimes not even try anymore. So, because students are failing in these environments teachers call parents in to talk about their children's poor performance. Parents trust the experts – principals, teachers, school systems, - to give them direction. But the experts have a one-size-fits-all approach that does not work for many young people.

In 1973, Roberta Flack sang "Killing Me Softly," a song that sums up where many struggling students are today. The verse and chorus are as follows:

"He sang as if he knew me
In all my dark despair
And then he looked right through me
As if I wasn't there
And he just kept on singing
Singing clear and strong

Strumming my pain with his fingers
Singing my life with his words
Killing me softly with his song
Killing me softly with his song"

"What is this song saying?" Well, I truly believe that our children's potential, passion, future and purpose are slowly being killed through the actions and attitudes of the American education system at large. Inadvertently, some of the methods our schools use to educate cause them to look right past the struggling students' pains, needs and concerns. They treat the classroom as if everyone learns in the same way. But every class that is not conducted in a way that acknowledges and addresses the different learning styles of children is negatively impacting their academic future.

On the one hand, our schools are telling our students that they have amazing potential, but then placing them in environments that do not acknowledge the uniqueness of each individual. Then we wonder why struggling students become apathetic and resistant to the educational process. We wonder why they begin to exhibit behavioral patterns that are negative and disruptive in the classroom environment.

Let me be clear. I am not here to bash public, charter or private schools. There are many students who are thriving in these institutions. I am attempting to explain what happens for students who are not thriving and to provide successful strategies to help them improve.

# The Problem

This book is written to parents and community organizations who would like assistance with developing and creating educational solutions for these students. This book is a resource for parents and organizations who desire to help students who think they are not smart, who have lost confidence in themselves and their abilities and who are struggling with their academics. I am here to help parents answer the questions these students may have like, What about me? What are my gifts? Am I special? How do I improve my academics? Why do I feel so dumb? Is something wrong with me?

Let me share a personal story to show my understanding of the problems and difficulties of having a struggling student. I will also give an overview of strategies that helped her win academically. Reading her story with reveal to you the heart and foundation for the strategies shared in the rest of this book. These strategies began with our children and expanded to many other students and families through several academic programs and coaching over a span of 30 years.

# STAR Finder

## *"Dannielle's Story"*

In our family, our daughter Dannielle struggled with reading. In fact, Dannielle did everything at a slower pace than her siblings. She felt dumb and her self-esteem was greatly impacted as she measured her weaknesses against others' strengths. What made it worse was that she had an older sister who was a high achiever and did well academically. It was heart-wrenching to watch Dannielle continually doubt her value and her own uniqueness. At times, I felt helpless and hopeless as a parent, wondering how to help our precious little one.

What could we do to help Dannielle find and develop her strengths while she struggled with academics and her perception of her own abilities? How could we convince her of her value? Well, we prayed fervently to God for an answer and we waited and waited. At times, I cried my heart out because the answers were not forthcoming. But over time, we learned how to develop a special place in our world that allowed Dannielle to shine. By observing the things that she had a true passion and love for, we could highlight her gifts and allow her to realize her worth.

We noticed the things that she did well in our home. For example, she was what we called the "Finder." If anything was lost in the house, we would always ask Dannielle if she had seen it. She would be able to view it in her mind and tell us where it was. She had visual strengths, and because she moved at a slower rate, she noticed and remembered things that others did not notice. We used this gift to help her to develop study skills that were visual and hands on, which made a huge difference in building her ability to retain complex information. Once we began to identify areas where she had specific strengths, we acknowledged those areas and praised her for them in public and at home. She responded positively to our efforts, but she was probably about 9 or 10 years old by this time, so we had some work to do to rebuild her self-esteem and to help her find her own identity.

We had a family tradition of celebrating each person's strengths, but we also had frank discussions about each of our weaknesses. And yes, this included mom and dad. Why? The secret for parents is that to lead our children and to help them with an area of struggle, we must be authentic ourselves. Our children know who we are. If we are not honest about our own struggles, we will eventually hinder the opportunity to help them with their own challenges because they will see us as hypocritical.

In addition, we will not have the insight to help them develop their strengths.

Dannielle had so many strengths. She loved animals and took excellent care of them. She became the animal expert in our home and was the sole caregiver of all our many pets. This created an opportunity for her to shine. She became the neighborhood animal expert. If a bird fell from a tree or someone found a turtle in the grass, they brought it to Dannielle to find out what to do. She always knew what to do or would research treatments and solutions. She was so good at caring for animals that she began to raise rabbits in our backyard and sold them to the local pet store in exchange for food and bedding for her other pets. She became better at reading and math because she needed to learn about her animals and expand her business.

Dannielle eventually became such an avid reader that in high school she owned a book collection of over 500 chapter books! She also improved her academics to the point that she graduated from high school with a grade point average of 3.1 and college with a grade point average of over 3.9. She is currently a phenomenal middle school science teacher whose struggle with academics caused her to create hands-on strategies to help her students connect with and better understand science. I believe her academic struggle helped her to envision how to assist her students to succeed. The very thing that was initially a problem became the thing that makes her better at her job. Dannielle also teaches general science, physical science, biology and chemistry classes to homeschool students. Her students love her hands-on, interactive, technology integrated classes, and at her recent middle school evaluation session, over 90 students gave her a standing ovation. Go Dannielle!!

## Strategy #1:

Take a week or two to observe your child. Look for any tendencies, interests or patterns that might indicate strengths. At the same time, try to discern the root of any academic issues your child is dealing with now. Maybe you've never thought about it before, but now is a good time to write down your thoughts and discover patterns.

## Strategy #2:

What areas of weakness do you need to talk about with your children so they will be more open to your help? This means your struggles – shared with discretion – and theirs.

How do you create a safe environment in your home that celebrates strengths and is honest about challenges so that your children will begin to see the areas in their own lives that are special and those that need to be improved?

"Your children's academic struggle may become their identity because everyone is so focused on it. Instead, remind your child that God does not see them through their struggle, He sees them through their potential – which is limitless."

~ *Mrs. Anita Gibson*

## *Chapter 2*

There are numerous reasons why our children struggle, but as a parent, you have more power than you think. Use this chapter to assess the things you are doing well and where you could improve. If you take the suggestions listed, I guarantee your child will be better equipped to succeed academically.

I was a very precocious little girl. My parents said I was always asking questions about things most children never even considered. I remember the answer to those questions were very important to me. For some reason, I needed to know the answer for my world to make sense. Now that I am an adult, I can understand how frustrating having me around probably was for my parents!

My dad was in the Air Force, so we lived in different countries and states, including Japan, the Philippines, Maine, Nebraska, Texas, Pennsylvania and Maryland. He was one of the first African Americans who enlisted in the Air Force, which meant that we were usually in the minority wherever we went. This was during a time when racism was very open and accepted. Even so, I loved the exposure to new cultures, the food, the beautiful places and the languages. But can you imagine what it must have been like for my parents to have a little black girl who was always asking them, their colleagues and sometimes random strangers questions? As I look back, I realize that I probably created some uncomfortable situations for my parents and others by asking questions about skin color, clothing, customs, food and the list goes on.

I wasn't shy, so I asked questions of anyone who would listen. I learned languages very easily, so I often understood what people were saying and would try to communicate with the locals. Now, if you asked my parents about how they were able to manage my constant questions as a child, they would tell you that it was difficult to handle such a verbal, communicative child. They would tell you that sometimes they just needed me to shut up! However, what they didn't realize is that the very thing that irritated them the most about me was an indicator of my gifting and future direction.

Did you just ask yourself if the very thing that irritates you about your child may be an indicator of future potential? Yes, that is exactly what I am proposing. Let me explain. Now that I have studied some of the StrengthsFinder™ research out there, I know that I have a strategic strength. I am always looking at the big picture, while trying to identify solutions to problems. I am also fascinated by how things work. Love of learning is another strength I possess. I love understanding why something exists, why it works in a certain way, how it can be used. So, the constant questions and conversation were (and still are) my attempt to understand and to know more.

What if my parents had been equipped with the knowledge that my inquisitive mind was an indicator of my future path and potential? What if instead of trying to squash that tendency, they acknowledged it as a gift, and then, taught me what boundaries were required for using it? What if they identified opportunities within and outside of our home to allow me to practice communicating? How would that gift have developed? Do you see where I am going with this? Now you may ask, "What does this have to do with being an academically struggling student? Well, I am glad you asked.

Students who struggle academically <u>always</u> have strengths in other areas. But in many cases, the academic struggle overshadows those areas. In the quest to solve the academic challenge, parents may overlook the child's areas of strengths, which are left unexplored or underdeveloped.

This is what many people don't realize. When a child begins to explore areas of strength, it provides confidence and highlights areas where the child shines. It opens doors to new opportunities and even helps to make it easier to address weaknesses because the child can focus on what he or she does well. This is a more balanced approach to working on academic areas of weaknesses.

Just imagine being able to see all the facets of your child – their strengths and weaknesses. Just imagine if you could redefine his self-image by focusing on what he does well and not just on what he does poorly. I will share more about the power of strengths later.

As you learn about these strategies, don't beat yourself up or feel like a failure. Although my parents did not have access to these resources, they did a great job with the knowledge and resources at their disposal. My dad taught my siblings and me about the importance of discipline, perseverance and humor. My mom taught us the social graces, encouraged our musical strengths and taught us life skills. I thank God for my mom and dad.

# STAR Finder

## "Sometimes What We Don't Know Is Part of the Problem"

Being a parent is no easy task. Dealing with an academic challenge as a parent can be difficult. As a homeschool parent, I felt lonely and hopeless at times. Sometimes I felt angry at my daughter. I would think, "She can do better. She just needs to stop being lazy or she needs to focus more." I got so tired of reviewing phonics over and over. She would finally get it, only to have to start from scratch the next day. She would look at me like I was speaking a foreign language.

I remember days when Dannielle cried tears of frustration, and so did I, because I could not figure out how to help her. We had days when we had to put the assignments away because we were not making any progress. Some days I felt guilty because I was impatient and unloving. Other days I used anger to control the situation, which only wounded her deeply. I learned more about my own ego, pride and selfish heart during those times. Some days I didn't like what I saw in myself and was shocked by how ugly it was. I had to do a lot of apologizing, and I prayed a lot, but I still wasn't perfect.

I wish I had been more emotionally intelligent, more spiritually mature. Sometimes I made it harder than it had to be. I wish I hadn't compared Dannielle, in my mind, to her older sister who started to read at 3 years old. I thought all kids learned like that. I didn't know what I know now; every child learns differently. I didn't know how beautiful my quiet, precious Dannielle was; that she had strengths in other areas that were just as amazing and incredible as her extroverted older sister, Lauren. But I learned. I learned that Dannielle had a huge heart and the gift of a nurturer. She was always taking care of the less fortunate, the underdog. I learned that Dannielle had all kinds of gifts and strengths, and she taught me the joy of being deliberate, taking my time and seeing the loveliness around me.

Dannielle taught me to see the glorious beauty of every child. I learned that God has a purpose and a plan for each life in the kingdom of God. I learned to be a child whisperer and to hear their hearts even when they weren't talking. I learned to speak to their hearts even when I wasn't talking by being intentional about my mindset and actions. I learned that God gives us just what we need. I learned that love is an action word and mommies need a lot of it. I learned that my children didn't owe me anything, and what I thought in the beginning was a sacrifice, was in the end, a privilege and an honor. God trusted my husband Glen and me to find their beauty as we learned to see our children through God's perspective. He gave us Lauren, our valiant one; Dannielle, our nurturer; and Ricky, our sunshine. It took me time to realize the treasure that we had been given, but I am so grateful that it didn't take too long. Did we do everything right? Absolutely not! However, we gave it our best, just as our parents had done before us. And we are so proud of our wonderful children. They have grown up to be amazing adults who love God, who love us and others and they are walking in their gifts with grace and confidence. Our children were the first to experience the S.T.A.R. Finder principles. Their success and the success of the many other students I have coached is proof that these strategies work. Let me share with you where our children are now.

Lauren, our oldest daughter, received a bachelor's degree in international marketing and a master's degree in international affairs from American University. She is an excellent Foreign Service Officer with the U.S. Department of State, and has served in Togo and Vietnam. Lauren is fluent in French and Vietnamese. When Glen and I visited Vietnam, we met the Vietnamese nationals who worked for Lauren, and we could tell by the things they talked about that Lauren was a gracious, kind supervisor.

She also has her own incredible travel show on Facebook and YouTube (www.facebook.com/countrycrushtv). Lauren has traveled all over the world and loves it because she is living in her purpose.

**Visible Pattern**: As a child, Lauren loved studying other cultures and told us that she was going to travel the world, and now that is exactly what she is doing.

Dannielle, our second daughter, received her bachelor's degree in elementary education from Bowie State University. She is a phenomenal, loved, and celebrated science teacher. She has an amazing ability to teach students in middle and high school General Science, Physical Science, Biology, and Chemistry in creative, hands-on ways. Even though she has high expectations, the students desire to meet those expectations. She has the ability to effectively transmit scientific knowledge to her students because she is flowing in her purpose. Dannielle also embraces her creativity, running an Etsy business that sells handmade crocheted and knitted products that are in high demand.

**Visible Pattern:** Dannielle loved all things about science and animals. She also had a gift of nurture which she used to care for her animals and to help those who were disadvantaged around her.

The youngest child in the family is our only son Ricky, who is married to the love of his life, Allison, an amazing wife and teacher. Ricky has a love for children that is transformative and is a great teacher in a private school. His students absolutely adore him and when they find out that I am his mother, they treat me like a celebrity, which screams volumes more about him than it does about me! He is a self-taught computer programmer and currently owns his own successful and highly sought-after photography business. As with Lauren and Dannielle, Ricky is walking in his purpose.

**Visible Pattern:** Since he was very young, Ricky has been interested in photography and cinematography, taking pictures and creating funny video clips with his friends. He is an amazing computer programmer instructor.

Our children are not perfect. Glen and I are not special, and our story is not unique. There are lots of families just like ours. I can't guarantee a secret formula that promises that all will turn out well. But what I can do is share principles we have learned that can be applied to your situation. Then, as you connect with God and ask Him to reveal what works for your family and for your child, He will give you direction.

## Parents Are More Powerful Than They Think

So, let's look at your child. Who is he really? What kind of things does she enjoy doing?

I coached one parent whose young son was always breaking household appliances, looking inside to see how they worked. His behavior frustrated her, so she brought it up at one of our coaching sessions. Well, I suggested that they visit the Thrift Store and encouraged her to allow her son to purchase several items that were interesting to him. He was told that he could take the appliances apart and explore to his heart's content. This approach allowed him to choose the items that he wanted to explore and even reverse engineer the appliances by putting them back together. Guess what was being revealed? This young man demonstrated strengths in engineering, a gifting which could be nurtured, but only once his parents realized that the irritating habit indicated strength in a specific area.

# STAR Finder

*"Your Child Has No Greater Advocate Than You"*

To give your child the support he or she needs, the next thing you must understand is that you are and will always be your child's greatest advocate. An advocate is one who publicly recommends or supports a person. A synonym is "champion," "spokesperson" and "fighter." If you are going to accept being your child's advocate, please realize that it is an important assignment. It means you will be required to make new sacrifices so that you can effectively get the job done.

When you are an advocate, you must become well known to teachers and administrators in your child's school. When the "experts" recommend medication or special needs classes, you need to do the research for yourself. When you realize the academic environment is harming your child's self-esteem, you must find another solution for him. YOU can decide when what is happening is not ok.

Some of our students are struggling with their academics because they are being bullied in their school or on social media. Studies show that a student who does not feel safe in his academic environment will struggle with learning. Some students become depressed because they feel trapped and don't feel they can say anything. Did you know there is an unspoken code that intimidates students into believing that no matter what happens in school, to say something is "snitching," an unpardonable sin in their peers' eyes? Don't assume it's easy for them to tell you what is happening at school. They can be intimidated into believing that when their peers find out, there may be serious consequences. They may fear that you cannot protect them from those consequences. That's why you need to be involved at school, know their friends and spend time with them.

Recently, a 15-year-old girl was raped on Facebook Live by five or six high school boys. Now that is tragic enough, but what makes it worse is that 40 people viewed the live broadcast and NO ONE called the police! When I asked some students about how they would have responded to the situation, they all mentioned the snitching code and said that they would have just turned off the video. Their response was heartbreaking!

Every day, your kids are a part of this school culture. They need you to visit their schools, to make it your mission to make sure they are okay. Pray as you walk down the hallways for God's protection of your children and their peers. Volunteer to help with school functions. They need a champion who will speak on their behalf. They need a parent who won't tell them to take care of it themselves because the truth is they don't feel they can and are not equipped to do so. They need someone who is bold enough to visit their schools unannounced to see what is happening.

# Parents Are More Powerful Than They Think

*"How Are You Monitoring*
*Your Child's Social Media?"*

Electronic devices and social media can be useful tools, but they could also be hindering your child's ability to do well in school because they can make it hard to focus on academics. Students who struggle with academics sometimes need to spend more time getting their assignments completed, but instead of working on their assignments, they fall prey to spending too much time interacting with their friends via social media. The brain needs time to be quiet, to think, to restore. Too much electronic usage causes a student's creativity and thinking process to pause and sometimes freeze.

All children are not ready to be fully responsible for how they access and interact with social media. Your children need you to be courageous enough to not allow them to have any social media accounts or phones that you cannot access (i.e. passwords). When was the last time you looked at their Facebook pages or viewed their Snapchat accounts or tweets? They may need your help navigating this space. In my opinion, this is not a trust issue. It's a maturity issue. Even though your student is in high school, it doesn't mean that she doesn't need guidance, especially with the questionable content that's available on the internet these days.

Be aware of the weapons of mass distraction that are all around us: television, Facebook, Twitter, Snapchat, gaming apps, etc. As parents, we have some of the same temptations as our children, but add in Amazon, Pinterest, email, sports, news, fashion sites and the list goes on and on. Statistics show that the average person checks his phone every 12 minutes![1] If we are awake for 15 hours on average, then we interact with our phone about 75 times per day and some people are looking at their phones more often than that! And that does not even include phone calls. We say we don't have time, but I don't think we realize how much of our time is being sucked up by the distractions all around us.

Stop feeling obligated to answer your phone every time it rings. Turn off those push notifications. Be careful of the amount of time you are just scrolling through social media. It's stealing time you desperately need to be available for your child. Do you realize how much more productive you are if you are not being constantly interrupted? It takes time to get back to what you were focusing on and sometimes

---

[1] Gregoire, Carolyn. (2015), You Probably Use Your Smartphone Way More Than You Think. Huffington Post.

you forget what you were doing all together. Are you fully present for your child?

How often do you "unplug" in your house? What do I mean? How often does your family intentionally put down the electronic devices to talk to each other? If you pick the kids up from school, do you have a few minutes to talk about their day? The truth is, most of us – parents included – are addicted to our cell phones. We all need to detox every so often. We can minimize the isolating, and potentially negative, impact of social media and the internet by scheduling "gadget free periods" every day. Start off with just 10-15 minutes daily, where you ask about your child's day with questions that require more than yes/no answers. Create healthy dialogue that leads to meaningful conversation. Find incentives that will encourage them to communicate with you. For example, "we will go get an ice cream cone if you can tell me one thing that happened at school today that you liked and one thing that astonished you, angered you or caused you to be upset." You would be surprised. Incentives go a long way!

Here are two more radical ideas for unplugging, first, commit to eating dinner without electronics at least twice a week. If you are not doing this in your family, then you are missing the important, informative and eye-opening conversations that naturally occur when you are eating with each other. A very important skillset will be learning to listen and not respond with facial expressions or comments. Just let them talk. This means no phones, social media, laptops or television. If you are saying to yourself, "my child won't talk to me," keep an open mind during this process. If you want them to begin to communicate with you, make some room. As the old saying goes, "if you build it, they will come."

Second, ask for your children's phones when you want them to prepare for bedtime and return them in the morning. Why? Because many of our children are up all night interacting with social media while they are supposed to be sleeping; and we wonder why they are so tired in the morning. This has a major impact on how well prepared they are to engage with academic content at school.

As an advocate, you must make time to not only ask if your child's homework is finished, but also do a thorough check to verify that it is complete. You must know what is going on with your child's social media to help them keep balanced which means that as a parent you must stay balanced with your own use of electronics so you can focus better on helping your child. I always say, "Don't expect what you are not willing to inspect." If you find a way to implement some of these strategies in your family you will find opportunities to connect with your child more deeply, to slow down the busyness and negative influence too much access to social media creates and find yourself able to enter a level of mindfulness each day that will help you navigate life's challenges better.

# STAR Finder

*"Don't Use Your Past to*
*Understand Your Child's Present"*

Please don't ever use the argument, "When I was your age." It is simply not relevant and that statement is more about you than them. They are individuals with completely unique strengths and weaknesses. Accept where your children are now. If they are not organized and are not keeping up with homework assignments, stop expecting them to fix it because you didn't struggle with it when you were their age. If they are struggling with their multiplication facts, even though you have gone over them so many times before, remember the struggle is telling you that additional assistance is needed. Accountability and a new strategy may be in order and you are going to have to take time to provide some level of support if you want it to get better. They don't have to fail to receive a wake-up call. Sometimes failure is necessary, but sometimes more parental oversight and support is what is truly needed.

There may be many reasons your child is struggling academically, but don't assume you understand the struggle. It might appear to be academic, but he may be dealing with a lot of things you never had to consider when you were in school.

### Strategy #3

Think about the things that irritate you about your child. Now, put on your coach's hat and see if those things could possibly be indicators of future gifts. What do you see? Why does the behavior bother you? Is it something inside of you that could be the real issue?

### Strategy #4

As your child's advocate, what can you do to start providing support or to increase the level of support?

### Strategy #5

What areas in your child's life need more accountability and/or consequences? Be honest.

"**How often do you _unplug_ in your house?**" ~ *Mrs. Anita Gibson*

# Schooling Should Not Be a Negative Experience

## Chapter Three

I'm sure your child's school is doing the best it can to ensure her academic success. Unfortunately, it may not be able to provide what your child truly needs. Parents have the privilege of being on the front line when a child is struggling academically. They are positioned to make a difference for that child in a way that even the school system cannot.

Here is what I mean. Over the years, I have coached many parents who realized that they needed to do something immediately to address their children's academic challenges. Many of these parents were tired of watching their students begin a new school year, hopeful that they would be successful, only to find themselves in January with the knowledge that their educational choice is not working!

By the time the parents got to me, they were so frustrated. They had already talked to the teachers numerous times to find out how to help their children. They had already met with the principal to share how their students were not being served well. They were already tired of the day-to-day grind, pushing and prodding their children to get out of bed in the morning because they hated going to school.

Other parents would share how they had to deal with their children becoming depressed, reticent and withdrawn because of bullying and harassment by other students. They knew that they had to do something about it. When a child does not feel safe in an academic environment it makes it difficult for him to learn. These situations led to frustrated students and parents who realized it was time to make bold moves on behalf of their children.

Learning should be a pleasurable experience. Your child should enjoy something about their academics and be excited about some aspect of his school. It is not okay for her to wake up every morning and dread going to school. The longer children remain in environments that are not serving them well, the greater chance they have of losing the opportunity to discover their true potential. Now, there will always be some subject or experience that they will not like. That is normal. But when the entire experience is negative and they don't want to participate, you have a problem and it must be addressed.

Does your child dislike math because he is not smart or is it because his teacher is not good at explaining it in a way he can understand? Have you ever observed the class your child is always complaining about? I have had students tell their parents that they are receiving a bad grade in a subject because the teacher has an accent that is hard for them to understand. Instead of telling the student to listen harder, get a tutor who understands how your child learns and connects well with them.

Why are you settling for such a mediocre academic experience for your child? If you struggled in school, you might think that this is the way it is. I'm here to say it does not have to be this way. There are other ways to ensure that your child receives an excellent education. Consider consulting with an academic coach to discuss specific academic strategies for your child.

**Strategy #6**

Sit down with your child and talk about what he or she requires to be successful in school. Write out what the perfect school environment would look like. This will help you to better understand how the current environment matches up to what is truly needed. How close is your child's current school to your picture? What must change?

*"The Sad Facts"*

Are you aware that in some states they are covering the graduation requirement by giving students a "Certificate of Completion?" This certificate indicates that the student has been in attendance in the public-school system for 12 years and nothing more. It is not the same as a diploma. It can't be used to enter the military or be used in place of a diploma. These students are going to have a difficult time finding the most basic jobs and they are poorly prepared to attend college. This is creating what some people call the "thirteenth grade" at many of our community colleges. This means that a large percentage of students entering community college are not ready to enroll in freshman classes and must take developmental classes to reach freshman requirements. These classes cost the same as the credit level classes, but credits are not awarded, which is a waste of money. A statistic in the state of Maryland reveals that 65% of students must take developmental classes when they enter their freshmen year of college.[2]

The issue is not that some students will need developmental classes to move forward, but that so many students need them. The National Assessment of

---

[2] Bowie, Liz. (2017). Thousands of Maryland high school student seniors must do remedial work for college. The Baltimore Sun.

## Schooling Should Not Be a Negative Experience

Educational Progress (NAEP) Report by the U.S. Department of Education highlights these deficiencies in our education system, identifying the struggles of high school seniors in math and reading at the national level. Among other things, this report revealed that graduation rates are at an "all-time high." However, as noted by former West Virginia Governor Bob Wise, "more diplomas without adequate math and reading preparation is not a formula for success for students or the nation." I am sorry, but something must change about the way we are educating many of our students, especially our children of color.

The report indicated that there is a significant achievement gap. Thirty-two percent of white students scored at or above proficient, while only 12 percent of Hispanic students and 7 percent of African Americans achieved the same scores. We must do better by all of our children, but we should consider the fact that, in the words of Governor Wise, "education is still not a balanced equation for all students." There are ways that you can and should address these deficiencies in the education system.[3]

---

[3] Waldman, Caroline. (2016). Nations Report Card Results: Large Percentage of High School Seniors Struggle with Reading and Math.

## Strategy #7

How well is your child doing with reading and math? Go to an educational supply store and find some grade level assessments to use with your child so you know for yourself. Hire an educational coach to assist you in setting up a plan for your child to succeed.

**"When you are training your child, please don't expect what you don't inspect."**

~ *Mrs. Anita Gibson*

## Chapter Four

As parents, we wear so many hats. In today's society, the pace is frenetic and keeps moving faster and faster. The moment we acquire another nifty gadget to save us some time, we use up that time with more activity instead of resting. The world around us demands that we respond to it like a task master that never sleeps, and our children are caught amid the madness, just trying to survive.

This may be hard to believe, but having a struggling student may be a good thing. I know it doesn't sound right, but sometimes God uses difficulties to get our attention. Sometimes He sets up things that force us to focus on first priorities like God, family, children and the home.

To truly help your struggling student, you must be strong and replenished yourself. You need to be rested so you can think properly. You need to have time to visit the school, talk to teachers and administrators. You need to find help to figure out strategies to work on academics at home. Simply put; it simply takes time.

This may be a season when you are going to have to say NO to some things. You must! You are the only advocate on which your children can depend. If you don't fight on their behalf to make the academic experience better, who will? Who loves them, knows them, and appreciates them more than you? God gave them to you because He knew you would stand up for them and help them become what He intended them to become. He is counting on you to get the job done. If the president of the United States asked you to take on a special assignment for him and it was a president you liked, what would you say? Probably yes. What if the assignment was very difficult? What would you say? Probably yes. Well someone a lot more important than that trusts you to help your child navigate his or her educational struggle. You may not have a degree in education, experience in certain subjects or be a child psychologist, but you have the amazing opportunity to become an expert on your child. All it takes is the will to make it happen and you will become a formidable champion for your student. But you must make this assignment a top priority.

Yes, you are a champion, a person who fights or argues for a cause or on behalf of someone else. As I shared in chapter two, several synonyms of a champion are defender, supporter, advocate, and fighter. Does your child feel like he has a champion, who is prepared to make sure he gets everything he needs to be what God wants him to be? You may not feel it yet, but you are reading this book because that is exactly who you are and you are ready to learn how to become the very best champion you can be.

God is using these academic challenges to help you see clearly just how to become experientially what you already are positionally. You must begin to nurture your children with intentionality and purpose from a place of strength, faith and trust in God. When He gives you an assignment, He gives you everything you need to accomplish it and accomplish it well. You may not know where all your resources are yet, but when you realize that they are available, you will start to look for and find them. You will realize that this academic problem comes with provision, promise and purpose. It's how God matures you. He is using your child's struggle to draw you closer to Him so He can give you the provision, what's needed to succeed; the promise, what He says about your issue; and eventually the purpose for the trial, the reason why He allowed it to happen.

Your life will change when you begin to understand that God's intentions for you are ALWAYS good! You must whole heartedly believe that He is working on you and your child's behalf, not based on the way your circumstances feel or the way it looks, but because He absolutely adores you. The Bible says that while we were sinners, Christ died for us. That means He gave up His life so that you and I might have life. He did it while we were His enemy. If He loved us enough to be willing to give His life when we were His enemy, how pleased do you think He is with us when we become His friends? When you receive Jesus Christ as your savior, God no longer sees you. He sees His son, Jesus. He sees what you and I are becoming and His Holy Spirit is always drawing us to desire to come closer and closer to God Himself. He is not angry with you, ever! He is not pointing an accusing finger at you like people may. He is lovingly drawing you to Himself by allowing certain situations into your life. He wants you to learn to trust that even though at times you (and I) do things that may disappoint Him, He will never leave us alone.

It's not that you won't _feel_ alone. But the truth is, you will NEVER be alone. He is working that truth into your heart day by day, trial by trial until you believe Him without inhibition; until you desire to live your life out of love for Him and not out of obligation or duty. Until you can see your child through His loving eyes without the need to receive anything back. He is working with you and me until nothing else matters, not other's opinions or desires, but only what He thinks about us. And eventually, you learn to delight in the fact that He is pleased with you and your desire to please Him above all else. The ability to have victory in this academic struggle is already yours because God knew before you and your child were born that you would need help. He doesn't trick you or make you figure it out. He has every answer you need, but you must learn to patiently wait on Him. The old folks used to say, "He may not come when you want Him, but He's right on time." Are you wondering if you can take it? Yes, you can. Are you wondering if you will make it? Yes, you will. The Bible says that if we seek the Lord with our whole heart, He will be found. I encourage you to ask Him to reveal what that means in your life and believe that He will answer you when it is time. Keep seeking, keep knocking and keep believing that His intentions toward you are good and for your good always.

You were made for this battle, so get on your armor, and with God's help, get ready to win! Become a champion for your child, the kingdom of God and His righteousness.

One of the strategies to become a great champion for your child is to first discover who God truly is. It is a life journey, but the more you discover who He is, the stronger you will become because you will learn who you are as well. Your strength and identity are directly related to learning through His word, the Bible, and experiencing who God is. He gave you strengths that are uniquely yours. Stop trying to be like someone else; value who God made you to be.

I know. Sometimes you look at yourself and think God must have made a mistake. Maybe you don't say it or even realize it, but if you hear yourself saying things like, "I wish I was___" or "I wish I had___" fill in the blank, then you don't understand how unique and intricate God's plan is for your life. Everything you need, He will provide. The question is not: do you have everything you need? The question is: do you know what you already possess? When you are acutely aware of what you possess in Christ, you can say like James in the Bible, *"I will count it all joy when I experience various kinds of trials, knowing that the trying of my faith works patience in me, but let patience have her perfect work (as I experience Christ through this trial) that I might become complete (I will grow and mature), lacking nothing." James 1:2-4NIV*

I have talked about God's role because He is the foundation to your success. You need a relationship with His son, Jesus. Not your ideas about Him, not what others say about Him, but a personal relationship with Him. Then, you need to connect with His word and His people, true believers (flawed though they may be). That is the key to where your power, patience, discernment, wisdom, perseverance and hope come from. That is how you make it for the long haul.

Now how does this help your child? Armed with a relationship with God, you must help your son to understand his own relationship with God. You must help your daughter to know that God is powerful and able to make her the best possible version of herself. As your children learn to totally and completely trust God, their academics will be positively and significantly impacted because God desires to help them, too.

I could have just given you strategies and my opinion on how to achieve academic progress; however, in my own experience, learning to trust and depend on God was foundational to my success.

# You Can't Pour from An Empty Cup

*"You Will Be More Effective If You Know Your Strengths"*

As a parent, your next step to helping your child find her true potential is to discover your own strengths. Then, you can use those qualities to help discover the best strategies to solve your child's academic challenges. You will also be able to identify the areas where you are weak and partner with other people and organizations, who demonstrate strengths in those areas.

Stop spending time trying to improve your weaknesses. Earlier in the book, I spoke about how a weakness will always be an area in which you are average at best. Improve your weakness enough so that it doesn't create an obstacle to success, but spend most of your energy on your strengths because you can develop them to various degrees of excellence. What are your strengths? Do you know?

One way to find clues is to answer the question, what would I do even if no one paid me? Then, think about the strengths, skills, etc. that it would take, and you will find clues to the answer. Another way to find out is to use an assessment that I love called StrengthsFinder™. It will tell you your top five strengths and provide a report that defines the strengths, how they manifest themselves in your life

and how to use them. Check out the assessment at
https://www.gallupstrengthscenter.com.

Knowing your strengths is very important as the parent
of a struggling student. You need to know if you are doing
the right work in the right way, as well as when someone
else is better equipped to assist. Once you know your
strengths, it will also help you to better prepare for
interactions with your child and others. Approaching your
child with an academic strategy that leans into your own
strength will help you to be more successful.

As you begin to understand your strengths and see the
positive impact that this information has on your own life,
you will be better equipped to help your child find his or
her strengths. This is another primary key in helping him to
grow from a struggling student to a successful one. You
will have greater, more positive impact on your child if you
are already familiar with your own strengths.

## Strategy #8

Complete the StrengthsFinder2.0™ assessment yourself
at https://www.gallupstrengthscenter.com. Once you
complete the assessment, pay a small fee to review the
report. Also, have your child take the assessment: Strengths
Explorer for 10 to 14-year-olds or StrengthsFinder 2.0 for

older students. Be sure to buy the NEW version, as the used versions will not give you access to the assessment. Even if the person selling it tells you it's NEW, don't buy it unless it is from the official website or Amazon.

The next step is to use a great resource that takes into consideration the parent and the child's strengths <u>together</u> and gives you strategies that will work specifically for your family. It's a book called *Your Child's Strength's – A Guide for Parents and Teachers* by Jenifer Fox.

Fox uses well thought-out plans, exercises and examples to help the reader learn how to re-focus their senses to work *with* children rather than trying to work *on* children. Her approach is designed to help the parent or educator guide the child in discovering his or her strengths. I'm sure anyone who has ever had or worked with a child can verify that truths which come from within are much more powerful and have much more staying power than those others taught to us. The book is a manual for recognizing our personal strengths, as well as enabling our children to learn to recognize and work with their strengths.

Fox is careful to explain both the theories behind this strategy and the actions needed to carry it out. The first part of the book explains the method and its successes. The second section defines and provides descriptions of the strengths, focusing on how parents and educators can use their sense to delve deeper, picking up on what children can't or won't say. The final chapters are a textbook with exercises, suggestions and charts each reader can use.

### Strategy #9

Write down your 5 top strengths, the definition for each one and ideas for how you will use them to develop strategies to help your child academically:

In our next chapter, I will introduce you to the S.T.A.R. Finder Revolution, which is the next key to help your children to succeed academically! Continue reading because "Help and Hope are Here!

**"Find the greatness in your child. Stop focusing on weaknesses; discover and celebrate strengths!"** ~ *Mrs. Anita Gibson*

## Chapter Five

Most of us were brought up with people focusing on our areas of weakness. They didn't mean any harm; their desire was to see us improve in an area that may have hindered us in some way. As a parent, I had to learn to reframe my thinking as our children were growing up. I remember struggling with the fact that Dannielle was not reading well in 4th grade. At first, I spent lots of time trying to "help" her read better, sitting right next to her as she tried to read her assignments, correcting the words (sometimes every other word) as she struggled to get through her reading book. Finally, her frustration and anger surfaced and the reading session ended abruptly. Then I too felt frustrated and like a failure because I didn't know what else to do!

I knew there had to be a better way. But what was it? My husband and I spent a lot of time in prayer, we talked with other parents, we picked our teacher friends' brains and a way forward began to emerge.

# How to Begin to Win!

*Reading Is FUNdamental*

We decided to focus on building her reading skills because I believe reading is the foundation to all learning. Think about it. What subject doesn't include reading in some way? Even in math, you must read and understand directions and be able to complete words problems.

I decided to restart Dannielle's reading journey by finding creative ways to reintroduce reading through fun and interactive activities. I no longer forced her to read each day. Instead, I would read chapter books to Dannielle and her siblings, including books like *Little House on the Prairie*, *Pilgrim's Progress*, *The Chronicles of Narnia* and *Redwall*. The choices were always above their grade levels, and I used sound effects and different voices for each character. I would stop the story just as something exciting was about to happen. My children would go off! They would beg and plead for me to continue, but I made them wait until the next day.

Eventually, I had to hide the books because they could not wait to find out what happened, and sometimes, I caught them reading in the dark under their covers at night when they should have been going to sleep. I had to pretend to be upset, but I was very happy that they were reading ahead to find out what happened. You may say, well I am not the dramatic type. That's fine, because you don't have to be! There are so many dramatized audio books available. Try a story on a topic that your child is already interested in and see what happens.

You may wonder, how did I get them to be so engaged with the books? We began the process by taking several small steps. You can use our journey as a roadmap for your own family. Plug in the things that work for you or create your own journey from scratch based upon your child's strengths and interests.

The thing that is the most difficult about this process is learning to lead by example. So, if you don't read regularly or don't enjoy reading, you will have an opportunity to grow in this important area with your child.

**Step #1.** Begin by creating "Delight boxes" or "delight areas." A delight box/area is a container or space that you can use to build activity experiences to draw out your child's gifts. It can be a box full of building blocks, instruction booklets or picture books that show how to build houses or cars. It could be an area full of art supplies, art books and a personal easel or a beginner robotics kit. It just depends on your child's unique interests.

## How to Begin to Win!

You don't have to know anything about these interests. The important thing is that these activities will begin to increase your child's critical thinking skills and will give them an incentive to read more. You can learn together, they can learn on their own or you can find someone in the family or your church with expertise or passion in the area and ask them to mentor your child. There just needs to be a process in place, which includes making sure they have a safe way to access the internet when they are researching (in other words, you should do the research together). The goal is to allow your child to develop his or her passion, a passion that is nurtured by in-home projects, special events and participation in relevant clubs or online groups. What you are doing is giving them a positive learning experience which will begin to rival the negative thoughts they already have about learning.

**Step #2**. Begin to plan family field trips in your area. We live in the DC Metro Area, and the great thing about living here is that there are many places to visit that are free. Before you go on a field trip, visit the library or go online to learn about the location so you can thoroughly prepare for your trip. You can even make research a fun family project!

Make sure to visit places that relate to your children's interests. If they love animals, visit a nature center, aquarium or local farm. Check out the volunteer opportunities and weekly or monthly programs in which your child can participate. This will really get them involved so they can be hands on with something they love. This will also enable them to develop their reading skills, reading about activities that they enjoy.

**Step #3.** Make regular visits to the library and to bookstores to allow them access to books at their reading level that are just for fun. This will enable them to connect with the material in new, more productive ways. As I mentioned, your children also need to see you enjoy reading a book. If this is a struggle for you, then it is an area that you must work to improve. The more you model the behavior you want to see, the more likely your child with model your behavior.

My kids and I loved the library. Every two weeks, we checked out over 30 books on all kinds of subjects that interested each child. I always checked out books about things that interested me, too. It was something we looked forward to with anticipation. I will tell you that we ended up with lots of library fines because we were not the most organized family. I think we probably have paid for a new library by now. But in the end, it was truly worth it.

**Step #4.** Use the "Technology Fast." As I mentioned in chapter two, this is when you limit the opportunities for your child to interact with phones, tablets, computers and television. Why? So that books and hands-on learning activities become more appealing. Sometimes our children will be better able to improve their reading skills if we limit the amount of time they spend using technology. We accomplish this by giving them opportunities to learn more about their gifts, passions, and interests. If we implement this first, many times they will naturally begin to decrease the time they spend on technology; although sometimes, they can use specific technology to explore their new-found passions.

Studies have shown that our brains do not function as well when multi-tasking. So, the next time your child tells you that he can complete his homework while watching television, you need to know that it is not true. More and more school systems are not allowing students to even bring their cell phones into the classroom because of the level of distraction their phones present.

Many people who own cell phones don't realize that they are addicted to their phones. Don't believe me? Just accidently leave your phone at home and it may be hard for you to focus while at work because the cellphone has become an integral, necessary part of your life. Well, the same goes for children. However, their need to interact with a cell phone may be having a negative impact on their reading abilities. How much time do your children spend on electronic devices? Take one week and keep track of how much time your child is interacting with electronics. You might be surprised at how much of their time out of school involves using these devices.

As a parent, you must be intentional about helping your child in the area in which he or she struggles, especially reading. Finding ways to improve reading skills must become a priority of your time and attention. Prioritize this area and I guarantee that it will get better. You can also use these strategies to help with other areas of struggle. If you think your child may have a learning disability it would be wise to have them assessed. Many school systems provide diagnostic services, I.E.P.s and various therapies to students who are having learning challenges. There are also organizations like Kennedy Krieger in Baltimore MD and others that can also provide assessments.

# How to Begin to Win!

We never told our children that we were going to stop watching so much television or back off the video games. We just started adding to our family life the activities that aligned with their gifts, passions and interests. In time, Dannielle began to see results. Finally, our struggling student's reading proficiency began to improve and soar.

It was so exciting to see her progress. When she was younger, we had her tested and her diagnosis indicated that she did not have any learning disorders, yet something was not clicking. We learned that sometimes a child just needs time. She may learn at a different pace and in a different way. If it's a maturity issue, that is something that you can't rush. While you wait for him to be ready discover what he is good at and what he enjoys.

If your child struggles in other academic areas, create opportunities to discover his gifts, passions and interests. Then, connect the area of struggle to those specific strengths. Find fun ways to learn math facts, use pizza to learn fractions, use a grocery store visit to work on multiplication and percentages. This is not meant to be an exhaustive list of learning ideas. It's meant to get you thinking about ways to help your struggling student to become better. There are so many programs available online. For example, Khan Academy or IXL Math are great online math resources.

### Strategy #10

Decide how you will use steps #1-4 to help your child to become more focused on the academic area in which he/she struggles.

In the next chapter, we will explore more about specific S.T.A.R. qualities that will add another layer to your child's success journey.

**"Don't let other people's opinions keep you from doing what's best for your child."** ~ *Mrs. Anita Gibson*

## Chapter Six

***STAR Finder*** is an acronym that stands for Strengths, Talents, Abilities and Resources. Each area is a vital component of the makeup of your student, and these components are keys to their uniqueness.

It is a new way for parents to think about their struggling students. I want parents to see that all students are truly *STARS* in one way or another. Each child shines in different areas that are unique and beautiful, just like stars that shine in the sky. STAR Finder gives parents strategies for celebrating and focusing more on what students have and less on what they don't have; on what they can do, not on what they can't.

The <u>S</u> in STAR stands for **Strength**. Strength is the ability to consistently provide near perfect performance in a specific activity.[4] The key to building strength is to first identify your children's specific interest. Next, show your children how to acquire skills and knowledge that relates to their interest, giving them space to nurture their gifts and grow their passion.

---

[4] Clifton's StrengthsFinder. www.strengthsfinder.com

# What is STAR Finder?

Let me give you an example. Dannielle demonstrated the strength of Developer.[5] It showed up in her love, care and nurture of furry animals. Her ability to nurture and train them was amazing; the good ones and the ones that were always getting into trouble! I am not crazy about animals in general, and especially not about rodents. Well, Dannielle decided that she wanted hamsters for her birthday. I was horrified! I thought, "What if they get out?!? Oh no! It's too much. I can't do it!" But then I realized that this was a unique opportunity for this child – who was struggling with academics and whose self-esteem needed a boost – to experience something that was positive and uniquely hers. Here was something that she was good at and had a passion for. Boy did I pray when she and her dad came home from the pet store with her first hamsters.

Their names were Mary and Jen Jen, and they were male and female. At that moment, I saw many hamster babies in my future! But when you are your child's champion, you put your desires to the side and choose whatever is necessary for that child to flourish. Let me tell you, I was terrified of rodents. I remember one incident, back when our children were babies. I heard a mouse scurrying around in a bedroom upstairs, and I went off! I

---

5 Clifton's StrengthsFinder. www.strengthsfinder.com

told my husband that if he didn't get that mouse out of our house that night, I was taking the kids and spending the night at a hotel. It got so bad that he had to call the church prayer line and ask them to please pray that the traps he set would catch the mouse because otherwise I was leaving! Well a little while after that call, we heard the snap of the trap and guess what it was? The mouse was caught! I breathed a sigh of relief, but it was too much stress!! I share this story to help you understand that the level of sacrifice involved in allowing hamsters in my house was huge, but it was necessary for Dannielle to begin to develop her passion and her gifts; her knowledge and skill. She ended up moving from raising hamsters to raising rabbits, and I began to get more comfortable with animals; just a little.

When Dannielle was 12 or 13, her gift of Developer continued to grow when she was offered the opportunity to create a tutoring program for a child in our neighborhood who was very smart but was born with facial deformities that required several surgeries. Her family wanted to protect her from children at school who might bully or harass her, but they also wanted her to begin a preschool program. Because Dannielle grew to gain a reputation in the neighborhood for being a smart young person who loved learning and was patient and kind she was asked to tutor this young girl. Dannielle created an amazing learning experience for her student. Her sensitivity, compassion and ability to relate to this little one and see her potential was truly amazing. We had the privilege of watching Dannielle's knowledge and skill in science increase, her passion for nurturing others grow and her gifts in crafts & design blossom. Her academic abilities also began to improve in every area. Looking back, we realized that Dannielle's strengths manifested themselves while she was still a child. But just imagine how you will be able to help your child if you can identify their strengths now and show them how to use them!

We used her strengths and passions to help her improve in reading, math, science and history. Her love of science and history was increased by finding fun, colorful library books about historical figures and scientists at her reading level, and taking weekend field trips to explore museums to experience the things that she learned about in the books. We would also visit the museum gift shop to find the perfect item to remember the field trip. Her strength of Input[6] kicked in there. She has always loved collecting things and insisting that each item had its own special place We would also create fun, hands-on projects that she would

---

[6] Clifton's StrengthsFinder. www.strengthsfinder.com

present to the family after dinner. She wanted to learn more about her animals, so her desire to read more about them increased. The desire to nurture others and the ability to transmit knowledge in fun and engaging ways began to become apparent. What's interesting is that the very thing she initially struggled with – academics – became the area in which she eventually excelled. I believe her struggle gave her more ideas, understanding and wisdom as she matured, and enabled her to apply those lessons to the benefit of others.

The **T** in S.T.A.R. stands for **Talents**.
Talents are your child's natural aptitude; feeling, patterns of thought, or behavior that can be productively applied.[7] Remember when I shared that Dannielle completed things at a slower pace than others because she was good at paying attention to details? Well, this was a blessing, as she was able to take in the details at a deeper level. If you asked her where the remote or hairbrush was located, she could tell you because her mind was taking pictures of her surroundings. She used this ability to develop an amazing talent to draw.

---

[7] Clifton's StrengthsFinder. www.strengthsfinder.com

# What is STAR Finder?

Dannielle made beautiful cards for special events and all sorts of lovely gifts, using paper, markers, clay, paints and other art supplies. We prepared an art box just for her so that she always had materials available to engage her creative side. Her heart to nurture others (i.e. empathy) enabled her to create gifts and cards to bless a lot of people in her world.

A talent can become stronger if knowledge and skill are applied and passion is present. Talents are innate, but can be improved to become better, if properly developed. Dannielle developed an amazing ability to draw because of her eye for detail. She could draw just about anything and was so good at it that people inquired about purchasing her work. We thought at one point that she might become a graphic artist, but she integrated her skills in art and her strengths in science and nurturing to create successful, hands-on learning opportunities and experiences as a teacher for her students.

The **A** in STAR stands for **Ability.**

Ability is the skill to be able to accomplish the fundamental steps of a task[8]. We had a rule in our home that everyone would learn to play the piano for one year, and then if they didn't like it, they could try another instrument. Dannielle had some natural musical skills and developed the ability to play the piano, but she wasn't crazy about learning the piano. So, she moved on to play the clarinet, which she found that she did not truly enjoy either. She had the ability to play both instruments, but because she did not enjoy them, she did not put in the time or effort to get better at it. So, it remained something she had the capacity to accomplish, but not something she enjoyed doing.

Now, her sister Lauren loved to play the piano and not only practiced her assignments, but was always trying to learn to play songs way above her skill level. In fact, she was so determined to improve that she would pick a difficult piece and spend hours on one measure of a song, which might only contain 10 notes, until it was perfect. This might take one hour for her to complete, but she enjoyed it so much that it did not matter. She developed this ability to the point that she became an accomplished

---

[8] Clifton's StrengthsFinder. www.strengthsfinder.com

pianist, who now, as an adult, still enjoys playing the piano as a hobby. See the difference? They both had ability, but passion drove one to add knowledge and develop skill for a hobby she grew to love and the lack of passion allowed the other sister to move on to discover what she was good at and apply knowledge and skill to that.

Although Dannielle did not enjoy playing an instrument, she had a wonderful ability to sing. She loved to sing and had a beautiful voice. However, because she was an introvert and shied away from the spotlight, she became uncomfortable when anyone asked her to sing and eventually stopped developing this ability because she did not want to be asked to sing in public. We are a musical family, so we have the privilege of enjoying her beautiful alto voice every now and then. It truly hurts my heart that the world will not get to experience the beauty of Dannielle's voice, but she had to decide what abilities she desired to develop and perfect.

Sometimes as parents, we push our students to experience things that we want them to try, not just because we see glimpses of talent, but because it's important to us. Maybe it's because we always dreamed of doing it ourselves or of having our child do this or that. Maybe it's because everyone in our family is supposed to experience it. Be careful to make sure that you motivate your child in the areas that they show inklings of strength, talent, ability and eventually desire. At first, you will not necessarily clearly see the unique blend that each of these areas will ultimately create, but as you allow them to continue to experience various things a pattern will begin to emerge.

Sometimes you will see glimmers of a specific gifting in an area that your children may not be interested in at the time. Be creative in finding ways to encourage them to try it anyway, even if just for a short period. We can see things that they may not be aware of yet, and sometimes they discover that what they thought they would not enjoy ends up becoming a delight. It's the same as when we offer them food that they have never eaten and they say, "I don't like that" and we say to them," How can you say you don't like it if you've never tried it?"

This reminds me of a time when, as part of an educational program I directed, we offered a public speaking class. One of the students in the class was so shy that she would literally cry when it was her turn to speak, and she would need some time to compose herself before every speech. She was mortified to speak in front of others, but she wanted to pass the high school class so she continued. Even though, initially, she was extremely nervous when she spoke in front of the class, over time she developed the ability to speak with great confidence and poise. Eventually, she was invited to speak to an audience of thousands at her church on a Sunday morning. This may not have been a strength for her, but with practice and consistency, it became an ability. This also caused her to excel in other subjects, as well, because she realized that with hard work, success could be attained in many areas.

When you are trying to discover your child's areas of strength, talent and ability, it is good to allow him to try several different things, even if he does not want to at first. Create an informal contract with him that includes the specific expectations. Once the agreed upon timeframe has occurred, if he still does not enjoy it or want to continue, encourage him to move on to try something else. It's good for your child to know up front how long he must do his best to explore this area. Be sure to explain what "best" means to you.

The **R** in STAR stands for **Resources.**

Resources can be categorized as assets that your children and your family have access to. They will enable them to improve their academics or expose them to other opportunities that are unique. Knowledge, relationships, assets, etc. that you as a parent may not have thought about; things that can have positive impact and make a difference in the life of your child.

For example, a resource could be knowledge or experience in a specific area or grandparents who have the financial ability to pay for a tutor. A resource could be a friend whose expertise in mathematics enables them to help your child after school or a church with a mentoring program that offers to help single moms raise their sons. It could be someone who can provide additional support by taking your child to horseback riding, piano lessons or basketball practice.

Resources are all around you, but you may not be aware of them or willing to ask for support. Other people may be available to help. They just need you to ask. Sometimes, when you are in the midst of trying to keep up with all of life's details, you don't think to reach out to others. You just try to figure it out on your own. Until recently, children have always been raised in a village, and many of you are finding out that it is critical, because the load is too heavy on your own. Ask God to give you wisdom and discernment to discover who else was meant to help you raise your child.

# What is STAR Finder?

In the past, people always lived with the family centered community concept. There would always be family members around or at least close by. Grandma or Auntie helped raise the kids. They could be counted on to babysit, celebrate birthdays and provide fun, educational activities and experiences. People knew their next-door neighbors and their neighbors shared their values. The neighbors helped keep an eye on the neighborhood children. In fact, they knew the children by name, and if they saw someone misbehaving, they would tell the parents. The school system allowed for prayer and supported the values that were being taught at home. There were at least four places (i.e. family, neighbors, school and church) that helped to raise children. This was our village. Unfortunately, parents move around more frequently these days and don't necessarily live near family, so they are lacking the built-in support of families. In addition, many people don't know their neighbors by name and sometimes not even by face. It's crazy, but some of us don't know what our neighbor looks like because they may enter and exit the house by the garage or work the late shift. You are not going to share your life or children with people you don't know or trust, so you just figure life out on your own.

The school system may not support your moral convictions and may even encourage your children to believe things in which you don't agree. Your child's school may not be serving him or her well academically. If you don't attend church, are struggling to find a church that is relevant or are not connected to other community organizations, you are also missing the opportunity to connect through youth programs, boy scouts and girl scouts, single mom support groups, etc. Then add to all this the fight that parents have with the media, which constantly tries to influence and mold your child into its own image for its own gain and you begin to understand the problem.

Now that you can see the differences in what was available in the past and what is available now to support families, you may begin to understand why raising a struggling student can feel so difficult. This results in parent fatigue and burnout. Do you see why you absolutely cannot try to raise your children without multiple systems of support?

## Strategy #11

In what areas do you need to offer opportunities for your child to explore her strengths, talents and abilities? What have you said no to because you are not comfortable with what you must give up or experience for it to happen? How can you turn that no into a yes?

## Strategy #12

Brainstorm all the possible resources that you and your family can access. Review strategies 1 to 12 in chapters 2 through 6, then prioritize them. Next, use them to prepare an educational plan for your child that is individualized and just right, enabling you to provide them with a plan to achieve academic success!

## Chapter Seven

You may have read Dannielle's story and thought, "that is all well and good, but I can't relate to it because that is not my child's story or you may not have realized that we homeschooled our children." I get that each child is completely unique, but you can still use principles from others' journeys to develop strategies to assist your student. My goal is to give you hope that no matter what your child's challenge, there is a way forward. In my case, it was homeschooling my children. Why? Because we wanted to be sure they would receive an individualized learning experience and we wanted to find a way to transmit our values.

Here are some homeschool academic performance statistics:[9]

- Students educated at home typically score 15 to 30 percentile points above public-school students on standardized academic achievement tests. A 2015 study found Black homeschool students to be scoring 23 to 42 percentile points

---

[9] Ray, Brian D. (2016). Research Facts on Homeschooling. NHERI

above Black public school students
(Ray, 2015).

- Homeschool students score above average on achievement tests regardless of their parents' level of formal education or their family's household income.

- Whether homeschool parents were ever certified teachers is not related to their children's academic achievement.

- The degree of state control and regulation of homeschooling is not related to academic achievement.

- Home-educated students typically score above average on the SAT and ACT tests that colleges consider for admissions.

- Homeschool students are increasingly being actively recruited by colleges.

When people think of educating their children at home, they generally express concerns about socialization, but home-educated students are typically above average when measuring their social, emotional and psychological development. Research measurements include peer interaction, self-concept, leadership skills, family cohesion, participation in community service and self-esteem. Homeschool students are regularly involved in social and educational activities outside of their homes, with people other than their family members. They are commonly involved in activities such as field trips, scouting, political drives, church ministry, sports teams and community volunteer work.

Not yet convinced? Think homeschooling is strange? Well, here are some examples from PXL Academy, a homeschool learning center that I developed for students who needed a small, individualized, hands-on learning environment. Three days a week, students are given 1-on-1 tutoring and participate in study sessions. Throughout the year they complete strengths assessments, activities and workshops. This program partnered with a homeschool oversight and group class organization called Shabach Christian Academy Homeschool, which also offered two days of classes in subjects like chemistry, biology, algebra creative writing and life skills, etcetera. The classes were taught by tutors with degrees or parents who had passion, expertise or experience in a specific subject area. They also provided administrative support for the parents, liaison to the state, field trips, guidance counseling and diplomas.

This partnership was a godsend for parents who worked full time or for parents who just did not feel comfortable or equipped to teach certain subjects. It gave parents the ability to give each of their students a learning environment that was conducive to their learning styles.

These types of programs have been in place since at least the 1980s, and as the statistics above indicate, they can be an effective choice for students who struggle academically. But there are lots of different ways to homeschool that can work for different budgets, family situations, etcetera.

Some homeschooled students work one-on-one with their parents at home, while other students also attend group classes in their area or participate in online classes in subjects like Creative Writing, Biology, Geometry and Government. The students may also have tutors for complicated subjects. There are groups that offer school picture days, holiday fellowships and proms, field trips, art classes, drama events, robotics competitions and lots of other classes and clubs, all with other homeschooled students. Students play sports with homeschool leagues, private schools and community organizations. Students can attend college while dually enrolled in high school, earning academic and athletic scholarships. In fact, many university and colleges are looking for homeschooled students because they tend to be good at learning independently.

I've made my pitch, but even if homeschooling is not the best option for you, the strategies included in this book will work for students in public, private or charter schools. This is where I come in as an educational strategist and coach. I help families create and develop educational plans that work for each student. I have access to resources for group classes, tutors, athletic programs, etc. While you as a parent are ultimately responsible for your child's education, as an educational coach, I come alongside of you to support and guide. I help provide information concerning the legal ramifications and the state requirements.

Here are some S.T.A.R. Finder success stories. The names have been changed to protect the identity of the students:

### Tony's Story

A student that I coached was in real trouble. He had failed 9th grade twice, and his mother was at her wits end. He was skipping school and hanging out with the wrong crowd. His behavior was becoming a problem, and his education was less and less important to him. Tony was on the path to becoming a school dropout. But then, his mom enrolled him in a small, hands-on homeschool learning environment. It took time for him to adapt to the smaller environments, but in the meantime, his mom found that he had a real interest in cars. He liked to fiddle with them. This new learning environment allowed him to fill in some foundational gaps, and he learned how to study and manage his assignment load. His love of cars helped him to stay on task with his studies because his mom promised that he would have an opportunity to get his driver's license, receive a car and start an automotive apprenticeship once he graduated. His passion was used as motivation to help him in his areas of academic struggle. When he began, he didn't care about his academic progress. But when he graduated 12th grade, he acknowledged that he was very thankful for the opportunity to rebuild his academic foundation and was very excited about his apprenticeship opportunity and new life. His transformation was amazing.

### Cory's Story

Cory entered PXL Academy both apathetic and angry. The traditional school setting did not work for him at all. The social and academic issues in that environment caused him to shut down, and his parents were frantically looking for another solution. This was going to be a challenge because he did not want to be homeschooled or attend our program. He was resistant to authority, and we were not quite sure about how to help him move forward. After a season of some ups and a lot of downs, we decided to give him some space to complete his assignments, while still partnering with his parents to find workable academic strategies and solutions. We continued to love him unconditionally and still held him to a high standard academically and behaviorally. Well, after a few months, he began to trust us. His academics started to improve and so did his attitude!

Ultimately, we attribute his success to lots of prayer and the powerful partnership of Shabach Christian Academy Homeschool and PXL Academy. The combination of these two programs brought a level of accountability and encouragement that helped Cory to release the old ways of thinking and consider what his future possibilities might be. He began to focus on his strengths and gifts, and his grades continued to improve. He even changed his original decision to skip college. He is now making plans to attend in 2018.

# Is Homeschool a Possibility for Your Child?

## Daryl's Story

Daryl was deeply depressed when he began attending PXL Academy. His family life was falling apart because his dad had abandoned the family and they became homeless. He was so devastated by his father's absence that he began talking about not wanting to live. At one point, he was admitted to Children's Hospital on suicide watch. He was in such emotional pain that academics were not a priority at that time.

He entered our program in the 11th grade with only around four high school credits. His mom could not get him to consistently complete his assignments and was at her wits end. She hoped that the one-on-one, individualized attention of our program would help him refocus.

One thing we noticed was that Daryl began to enjoy being able to play basketball with the other students during the lunch break. It became the highlight of his day. His mother told us that he did not usually participate in sports, but we noticed that PXL Academy's individualized, hands on environment allowed him to begin to improve academically. He developed friendships with several of the students and became more diligent with his studies. He began to enjoy the success he felt from completing his school work, which motivated him to do more and more.

He became quite a comedian and enjoyed getting his peers to laugh, which was sometimes a good thing and at other times not so good! But we lovingly helped him learn when it was appropriate to bring on the laughs.

Daryl had a love for the arts, so we allowed him to apply this interest to some of his assignments through special projects. After spending a year with us, the following school year he was accepted into a private school that allowed him to focus on the arts. He is doing well and is becoming an independent and diligent learner. Project Excel Academy lovingly and prayerfully provided the right environment for Daryl to be able to get back on track.

## Joseph's Story

Joseph was a good student, but his grades began to slip in his 10th grade year at a private school. The class sizes were increasing to over 25 students in each class. His math teacher was unable to set aside time to help him as he began to struggle with algebra, and he felt like he was getting lost in the shuffle. Joseph's parents decided that he needed a smaller learning environment where he could receive more one-on-one assistance, so they decided to homeschool him. He was enrolled in Shabach Christian Academy Homeschool and Project Excel Academy to make sure he received access to classes, one-on-one tutoring, accountability and studying sessions. It was just what he needed. He could have his questions answered and enjoyed being able to focus on his academics. He was academically strong and an excellent example to the other students of how to become more independent. He showed them how to take responsibility for completing their assignments. He was a leader among his peers and would encourage them to get back on track when they lost focus. His parents have been so pleased with his performance that they have already indicated that he will complete his 12th grade year in our program. He is an excellent student and is prepared to move on to an institution of higher education next year. He will be concurrently taking high school and college classes in his 12th grade year.

### Randy's Story

Randy was kicked out of a private school in 10th grade because of his behavior. Our program was his last chance. We let him know that disrespect to authority would not be tolerated; that we would help him if he remained self-controlled. He started off well, but we had a few issues that had to be dealt with along the way. Unfortunately, as he was beginning to make progress, his father and mother separated and moved apart. This disrupted his world emotionally, physically and spiritually. Because he now lived in two households, he began losing and misplacing assignments and would forget to turn in projects. Randy began to wonder if God cared about him. We realized he needed additional resources during this difficult time, so we increased his academic support to help him stay focused on his school work by providing additional tutoring and oversight support.

This was a two-year process for Randy, and at times, we were not sure if he was going to make it. Because the life issues caused him to lag academically, he had to go to summer school so he could graduate from 12th grade. We provided additional support at Project Excel Academy to help Randy complete his graduation requirements. Thankfully, he did finish by August and enrolled at Prince George's Community College that fall. He passed the entrance exam, and was at the college level with all but one of his classes. He was also recruited by the baseball team. His first semester was a little shaky, but Randy made a difficult choice and quit the baseball team so he could focus on his grades. This choice allowed his second semester grades to improve. and Randy is doing well in his first year of college. His story could have turned out very differently. We are thankful for his success.

We are very proud of our student's successes. They have positioned themselves to become positive forces and game changers in our world.

"**Don't use your past to try to understand your child's present. There is no comparison.**" ~ *Mrs. Anita Gibson*

# How Can Your Organization Create Programs to Help Students Succeed?
## Chapter Eight

One of the things I say all the time is "Help and Hope are Here!" The fact that our communities have students whose needs are not being met by traditional educational options is not the end of the story. There are many things that we can do to make a difference in the lives of these students. We absolutely can make a difference; in fact, we have an obligation to find solutions. These solutions should fit your organization's mission, resources and commitment level, but there is something that almost everyone can do.

As an educational strategist, I have a passion for helping families and organizations find academic solutions and tools that can help. What if organizations in our community decided to adopt a different school and then took responsibility for supporting the struggling students and their parents with the resources that would enable them to succeed? What if someone could give you a road map to show you how to make it happen? Here are some ideas to get you started:

*Idea #1*: Offer to financially support a tutoring program at your local public, private or charter school or support an organization that is already doing this.

*Idea #2:* Develop a tutoring program for students during the weekends or after school. Check to see if retired teachers are available to become volunteer tutors.

*Idea #3:* Use classroom spaces to host homeschool group classes and/or offer a homeschool administration program. If you are able, offer the space for free. Please contact me for more information about how to develop a program in your area.

*Idea #4:* Recruit mentors to serve with an organization that has established a mentoring program. Commit for the next year to impact youth for good on a weekly basis.

*Idea #5:* Make a commitment to tutor or to help your grandchildren, young family members and/or friend's children with their homework.

*Idea #6:* Check out ChurchAdoptASchool.org., a national program created by Dr. Tony Evans, and see how your church can get involved.

When you look at the ideas above and find yourself saying, "I can do that or "That's possible. It's not too hard," perhaps you are being called to make a difference for the students in your world. Let the S.T.A.R. Finder revolution begin! We don't have to wait on a government program, an organizational grant or anything else.

We have the resources within our communities right now, and with God's help we can make a difference. Not tomorrow, but today. If you are ready to make a difference in your community, please call me to set up a time to discuss the possibilities. If we don't do this, who will? Who's waiting on you?

Remember – "Every child is a STAR! Each of them have been gifted by God to be great at something. Sometimes you can see what it is right away, sometimes you have to dig a little." ~ *Mrs. Anita Gibson*

# STAR Finder Strategies

**Strategy #1:** Take a week or two to observe your child. Look for any tendencies, interests or patterns that might indicate strengths. At the same time, try to discern the root of any academic issues your child is dealing with now. Maybe you've never thought about it before, but this is a good time to discover and document patterns.

**Strategy #2:** What areas of weakness do you need to talk about with your children so they will be more open to your help? This means your struggles – shared with discretion – and theirs. How can you create a safe environment in your home that celebrates strengths and is honest about challenges so that your children will begin to see the areas in their own lives that are special and those that need to be improved?

**Strategy #3:** Think about the things that irritate you about your child. Now, put on your coach's hat and see if those things could possibly be indicators of future gifts. What do you see? Why does the behavior bother you? Is it something inside of you that could be the real issue?

**Strategy #4:** As your child's advocate, what can you do to start providing support or to increase the level of support?

**Strategy #5:** What areas in your child's life need more accountability and/or consequences? Be honest.

**Strategy #6:** Sit down with your child and talk about what he or she requires to be successful in school. Write out what the perfect school environment would look like. This will help you to better understand how the current environment matches up to what is truly needed. How close is your child's current school to your picture? What must change?

**Strategy #7:** How well is your child doing with reading and math? Go to an educational supply store and find some grade level assessments to use with your child so you know for yourself. Hire an educational coach to assist you in setting up a plan for your child to succeed.

**Strategy #8**: Complete the StrengthsFinder2.0™ assessment yourself at https://www.gallupstrengthscenter.com. Once you complete the assessment, pay a small fee to review the report. Also, have your child take the assessment: Strengths Explorer for 10 to 14-year-olds or StrengthsFinder 2.0 for older students. Be sure to buy the NEW version, as the used versions will not give you access to the assessment. Even if the person selling it tells you it's new, don't buy it unless it is from the official website or Amazon.

The next step is to use a great resource that takes into consideration the parent and the child's strengths <u>together</u> and gives you strategies that will work specifically for your family. It's a book called *Your Child's Strength's – A Guide for Parents and Teachers* by Jenifer Fox. Read chapter four for detailed information on this resource.

**Strategy #9:** Write down your top five strengths, the definition for each one and ideas for how you will use them to develop strategies to help your child academically.

**Strategy #10:** Decide how you will use steps #1-4 in chapter five to help your child to become more focused on the academic area in which he/she struggles.

**Strategy #11:** In what areas do you need to offer opportunities for your child to explore her strengths, talents and abilities? What have you said no to because you are not comfortable with what you must give up or experience for it to happen? How can you turn that no into a yes?

**Strategy #12:** Brainstorm all the possible resources that you and your family can access. Then, review and prioritize the above strategies. Next, use them to prepare an educational plan for your child that is individualized and just right, enabling you to provide them with a plan to achieve academic success!

# The Author

Anita Gibson is a **speaker, life coach and educational strategist**. Since 2002, she serves her community by introducing youth, women and families to a purpose-filled journey by helping them with to discover their strengths and how to use those strengths to achieve success. She teaches that each person's strengths are indicators of their future possibilities.

Many of her clients have shared that the safe and productive environment created through Anita's coaching has helped them achieve goals and accomplishments far exceeding anything they ever thought possible.

Anita has also served as a speaker for various youth events, graduations, women's ministry programs and parent organizations. She is known for her authenticity and transparency. Her desire is to show each person how to find their S.T.A.R. qualities (standing for strengths, talents, abilities and resources.)

She is the president of **Creative Strategies Consulting** that creates and develops educational programs for churches and educational organizations, and **PXL Academy**, an academic learning center for youth in Bowie, Maryland. The students enrolled have experienced major improvements in their academics and study skill discipline. Her motto is Help and Hope are Here!

# The Author

Anita Gibson resides in Maryland with her amazing husband, Glen. They are the parents of three adult children, Lauren who is a Foreign Service Officer, Dannielle, a middle school science teacher and Ricky, a computer programming instructor and professional photographer.

Anita's contact information:

Email: anita@anitagibson.com

Website: www.anitagibson.com

Twitter: www.twitter.com/AnitaGibsonEdu

Facebook: https://www.facebook.com/anita.gibson.391

Made in the USA
Columbia, SC
25 August 2017